The Composer

Kaylene Vasquez-Rodriguez

ISBN 979-8-89130-579-3 (paperback)
ISBN 979-8-89130-580-9 (digital)

Christian Faith Publishing
832 Park Avenue
Meadville, PA 16335
www.christianfaithpublishing.com

Printed in the United States of America

To my beloved son Josiah, whose laughter fills my heart with joy, a leader like Moses, whose wisdom and compassion inspire us all. Your resilience and determination are a testament to the strength within you. Remember what the Lord told Moses, "Now go; I will help you speak and will teach you what to say." Exodus 4:12

To my dear son Jerel, whose curiosity and imagination inspire me endlessly, with the strength and wisdom akin to Aaron of old, leading by example and showing unwavering faith.

To my precious daughter Kensley, whose innocence and love remind me of life's beauty every moment; reminiscent of the prophetess Miriam, your compassion, wisdom, and worship inspire us all, nurturing hearts and minds with your gentle touch.

To my husband Jeffery, whose steadfastness and compassion embody the spirit of love and sacrifice, much like the biblical figures who walked before us.

To my mother Magali, whose boundless love and wisdom have shaped me into the person I am today, a testament to the enduring power of a mother's love.

To our pastors, Angel and Angela Muniz from Iglesia Cristiana Damasco Pentecostal, whose guidance and spiritual leadership have enriched our lives beyond measure. your guidance and teachings have illuminated our path, leading us closer to God's divine purpose with each step we take.

This book is dedicated to each of you for the roles you play in shaping our lives and the love that binds us together.

To all the amazing children we know, whose hearts and spirits shine with the extra special touch of God's love. You are each a beautiful gift to the world.

The day we brought you home, our hearts sang a new song to God.
Our hearts played a melody that praised His name.
It sung of His wonders and majesty.
The melody added to the song your siblings had begun before you were knitted in my womb.
Ten fingers and toes, a sweet smile to match, and a belly full of laughter, song, and praise.
You were sent with joy, purpose, and dreams.

Your tiny hand cradled my face, and I asked myself, "How can the tiniest image of God impact me so much?"

You were perfect in our eyes, and forever shall you be.

Months passed; and our song at times paused, skipped, and scratched.

But deep down inside, I still knew it was our own.

Appointments, hospital stays, doctor reports, long nights of worrying… All that soothed was our bended knees at your bedside.

It was then we understood our composer was creating a symphony of all your unspoken words.

*****

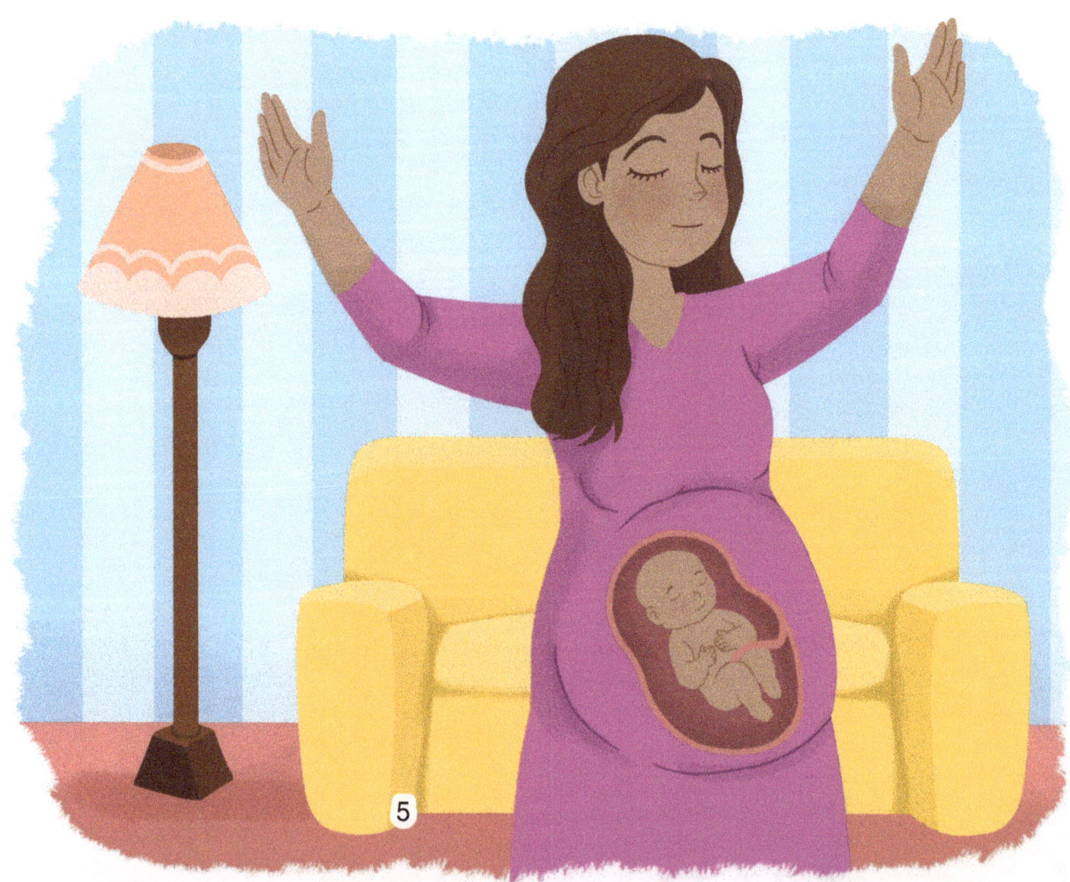

"Hi, baby. What's your name?" people ask.

No words come out…

For although You, oh Lord, know the words before they are on our tongues, the conversations are just between You and our baby for now.

You use your eyes to say, "Hello!"

You use your AT device to share your name.

*****

You added depth into our family's song that changed our lives forever.

Our composer had created a masterpiece.

When people would say, "You can't," Jesus says, "You can." And you did!

When your way of speaking is babbling, shouting, and pushing buttons on your AT device.

When people look your way, you turn away and, oftentimes, reject their touch.

When your way of talking is using your hands and facial expressions and you are left with a sense of frustration because you are still not understood.

Getting around may mean using a wheelchair or a walking cane.

When your physical eyes are not able to see yet, God created a world of pictures in your mind for just you and Him.

Maybe you are made to feel like an outcast because you prefer to play alone.

When your favorite hobby is lining up your car toys throughout the day.

When you can't eat what everyone else eats.

You are still part of God's symphony.

When your body has the wiggles and you can't sit still.

When loud noises upset you.

When words and numbers begin to dance on the pages and you can't make sense of them.

Your praise still reaches the one who saw you first.

In the sweetest of ways, you speak of His ways in your wonders.

And we continued to stay at our father's feet in hopes for an answer of who you would be.

I later understood that the work that needed to be done was in me.

And on that day, everything we thought you needed was given to us.

Our eyes and ears were opened. And we could hold and embrace all He had created in you.

I failed to realize that our composer had already created the most perfect of symphonies.

Just like Daddy and I, there are moms and dads who are praying the same prayer as ours. It is my hope that they, too, can hear the new song composed solely for you and your family.

Every one of you has been given your talents, your own strengths, and your own qualities so that God would be glorified through His masterpiece.

You were chosen to bring glory to God's name.

And His disciples asked Him, saying, "Rabbi, who sinned, this man or his parents, that he was born blind?" Jesus answered, "Neither this man nor his parents sinned, but that the works of God should be revealed in him." (John 9:2–3 NKJV)

Now go on and reveal the work of the Father!

About the Author

Kaylene Vasquez-Rodriguez—a wife, a mother to three, and a graduate student at Hunter College's special education program—demonstrates her expertise as a skilled content creator with a wide range of knowledge in various fields such as childhood education, learning disabilities, Christianity, and biblical principles. She excels in crafting engaging pieces that capture her readers' attention, specializing in narratives that educate, entertain, and inspire. Kaylene knows firsthand what it is like to be a parent to a child with a classification given by doctors. As a teacher, she works hand and hand with parents and students to ensure their voices are heard and represented. She now embarks on including that representation in the kingdom of God in the homes of Christian families, reminding families that their child is still part of God's symphony. It's evident that Kaylene genuinely loves what she does, and her enthusiasm shines through in her work.